3V

KT-239-187

700023809756

GROUNDBREAKERS

Sir Walter Raleigh

Shaun McCarthy

Heinemann
LIBRARY

H **www.heinemann.co.uk**
Visit our website to find out more information about **Heinemann Library** books.

To order:
☎ Phone 44 (0) 1865 888066
📄 Send a fax to 44 (0) 1865 314091
💻 Visit the Heinemann Bookshop at www.heinemann.co.uk to browse our catalogue and order online.

First published in Great Britain by Heinemann Library,
Halley Court, Jordan Hill, Oxford OX2 8EJ,
a division of Reed Educational and Professional Publishing Ltd.
Heinemann is a registered trademark of Reed Educational and Professional Publishing Ltd.

OXFORD MELBOURNE AUCKLAND
JOHANNESBURG BLANTYRE GABORONE
IBADAN PORTSMOUTH (NH) USA CHICAGO

© Reed Educational and Professional Publishing Ltd 2002
The moral right of the proprietor has been asserted.

All rights reserved. No part of this publication may be reproduced, stored in a retrieval system, or transmitted in any form or by any means, electronic, mechanical, photocopying, recording, or otherwise, without either the prior written permission of the publishers or a licence permitting restricted copying in the United Kingdom issued by the Copyright Licensing Agency Ltd, 90 Tottenham Court Road, London W1P 0LP.

Designed by AMR
Illustrated by Art Construction
Originated by Ambassador Litho Ltd
Printed by Wing King Tong

ISBN 0 431 10488 3
06 05 04 03 02
10 9 8 7 6 5 4 3 2 1

British Library Cataloguing in Publication Data
McCarthy, Shaun
 Sir Walter Raleigh. – (Groundbreakers)
 1.Raleigh, Sir Walter, 1552?–1618 2.Explorers – England –
 Biography – Juvenile literature
 1.Title
 942'.055'092

WORCESTERSHIRE COUNTY COUNCIL	
975	
BfS	11 Mar 2003
JB RALEIGH,W	£ 11.50

Acknowledgements
The publishers would like to thank the following for permission to reproduce photographs:
Bridgeman Art Library: pp. 9, 11, 13, 14, 16, 17, 24, 26, 32, 37; British Library: pp. 28, 29; Collections/Brian Shuel: p. 21; Collections/George Wright: p. 25; Collections/Yuri Lewinski: p. 8: Collections/James Bartholomew: p. 34; Corbis: p.15, p. 33; Fotomas: pp. 5, 10, 30, 36, 40; J. Batten: p. 7; Mary Evans: p. 19; Michael Holford: p. 20; National Gallery of Ireland: p. 22; National Maritime Museum: p. 31; National Portrait Gallery: pp. 4, 12, 18, 38, 41; Sherborne Castle: p. 23; South American Pictures: pp. 27, 35; Tate: p. 6.

Cover photograph reproduced with permission of Bridgeman.

Every effort has been made to contact copyright holders of any material reproduced in this book. Any omissions will be rectified in subsequent printings if notice is given to the publishers.

Our thanks to Christopher Gibb for his comments in the preparation for this book.

Disclaimer
All the Internet addresses (URLs) given in this book were valid at the time of going to press. However, due to the dynamic nature of the Internet, some addresses may have changed, or sites may have ceased to exist since publication. While the author and publishers regret any inconvenience this may cause readers, no responsibility for any such changes can be accepted by either the author or the publishers.

Any words appearing in the text in bold, **like this**, are explained in the glossary.

Contents

Note Many writers now drop the 'i' in Raleigh's name, spelling it 'Ralegh'. This is thought to be the way he would have spelt it. This book keeps to the traditional 'Raleigh' throughout.

The paragon of his age

ÆTATIS SVÆ 3
AN 1588

AMOR ET VIRTVTE

Raleigh as a young man. This portrait (by an artist identified simply as 'H') is designed to show off Raleigh's looks, his clothes, and (in the crescent moon in the background) his skills of exploration and writing poetry.

A few figures in history seem to sum up the spirit of the age in which they lived. Sir Walter Raleigh is regarded as the supreme example of the heroic, courtly adventurer and artist from the golden age of Queen Elizabeth 1.

A darker side

Raleigh mixed the energy of a seafarer and soldier with the refined manners of a **courtier** and royal favourite. He was intolerant of other nations, despised **Catholics**, had the aggression of a professional soldier, but wrote lyric poetry. He was intensely ambitious, always striving to acquire wealth, power and influence. His ships openly engaged in **privateering** and he amassed a fortune from this licensed **piracy**.

Raleigh was granted 'licences' by the adoring Queen, which allowed him to raise taxes from the population of England. He did this greedily and, in the middle years of his life, was hated by many ordinary people. He was proud to have taken part in a brutal massacre of Irish rebels and civilians that shocked even his contemporaries in a violent age. Although it is a mistake to try and judge a man living in the 1500s by our own standards, it is undeniable that he could be ruthless and violent. His enemies nicknamed him 'That Great Lucifer'.

A man of his time

Raleigh was unfortunate in that he lived beyond the age that valued his talents. When Elizabeth I died and James I came to the throne, Raleigh was suddenly out of favour. He was twice imprisoned, and finally executed for **treason**. While Elizabeth ruled, war with Spain, and hatred of any Catholic country in Europe, were the order of the day. Raleigh continued to use his ships to attack the Spanish in the Caribbean in James's reign, while the new king was trying to make peace with the Spanish.

Yet in the last years of his life, many people again admired the dashing, heroic figure imprisoned in the grim **Tower of London**. Raleigh may have reminded people of the 'golden days' of Elizabeth's reign, but his arrogance, pride and sometimes reckless adventuring belonged to an age that had died with the queen who had so adored him.

Raleigh's life and character reflect the extremes, from poetry and fine manners to wars and executions, that typify English exploration and discovery in Elizabethan times.

Raleigh spent at least as many years of his life writing books and poetry as he did adventuring. This is the ornate title page from his massive History of the World *that he wrote while in prison.*

THE
HISTORY OF
THE WORLD.

In Fiue Bookes.

1. Intreating of the Beginning and first Ages of the same from the Creation vnto Abraham.
2. Of the Times from the Birth of Abraham, to the destruction of the Temple of Salomon.
3. From the destruction of Ierusalem, to the time of Philip of Macedon.
4. From the Reigne of Philip of Macedon, to the establishing of that Kingdome, in the Race of Antigonus.
5. From the setled rule of Alexanders successors in the East, vntill the Romans (preuailing over all) made Conquest of Asia and Macedon.

By Sir Walter Ralegh, Knight.

A Devon boyhood

Walter Raleigh was born in 1554. His father (also called Walter) was a successful farmer and ship owner who was an important figure in **West Country** society. His mother, Katherine Champernowne, was the widow of another West Country landowner, Otto Gilbert. She had three sons by Gilbert, named John, Humphrey and Adrian, who all became successful political or seafaring figures. But none approached the fame of Walter Raleigh.

This 19th century painting of young Raleigh listening to an old sailor's tales is an idealized portrayal of the romance of his Devon childhood. In reality the proud Raleighs would probably not have wanted to talk to an old sailor!

Devon seafarers

The West Country, and Devon in particular, was far more important and influential in Raleigh's time than today. Ships, for **privateering**, trade and voyages of discovery, were vital to England's dream of expansion and power. Devon had many ports and a history of skilled seafaring. Walter grew up at Hayes Barton, near Exmouth, where his father kept privateers.

The gentlemen of the west

The 'gentlemen of the west' were a group of Devon men with political or seafaring interests, who controlled much of the county's economy.

Raleigh's boyhood home is amid the peaceful, rolling hills of East Devon, but it overlooks the Channel where his father's privateers roamed.

With Devon being so remote from London (260 kilometres or 160 miles by muddy tracks, impassable for months at a time), the gentlemen of the west effectively ruled over local people. They were fiercely **Protestant** and dealt violently with any attempts to promote the **Catholic** faith in the West Country.

In 1549, Raleigh's father helped crush a rebellion by local people who wanted freedom to worship how they wished, and who questioned the power of the gentlemen of the west. At its bloody end, 4000 Devon men lay dead in the fields around Exeter (then the county town of Devon).

Early influences

Walter was probably given lessons in seafaring by his father and half-brothers, and a grim lesson in active politics was arranged in 1569 when it was decided he could go to France with a group of other young West Country gentlemen to fight alongside Protestants who were at war with Catholics. Raleigh was just fifteen years old, but experience of warfare was considered part of a gentleman's education at this time.

The cruelty Raleigh experienced in France might have hardened his attitude to fighting and helps explain some of his later violence, especially against Catholics.

> **On the horrors of war:**
>
> *'[A place] where murder is no cruelty ... [where people] were bathing in one another's blood, making it custom to despise religion and justice ... amid barbarous murders, devestations and other calamities ...'*
>
> (in the words of an English volunteer)

War, education and a voyage

In Raleigh's time, Europe was divided by religion. Italy, Spain France and Portugal were **Catholic**, England and most countries in Northern Europe were **Protestant**. Both sides used religion to gain support for their political or military plans. Spain, for example, wanted to invade England during Raleigh's time, not just to conquer the country, but also to convert the population to Catholicism. Many countries feared wars that were caused by religious differences and they did not tolerate people who did not follow the religion of the monarch and government.

Raleigh thought hard about what he saw in France. Aged just eighteen, he wrote that the French Religious War had been 'begun and carried out by some few great men of ambition and turbulent spirits, deluding the people with the cloak and mask only of religion, to gain their assistance'. In other words, he realized how ambitious men used religion to make others help them to achieve power.

Education

As the son of a gentleman, Raleigh was sent to Oxford University after his return from France in 1572. He left after three years without gaining a **degree**. Reports suggest he was considered 'very proud' by fellow students and not overawed by the grand old university. He was already revealing his characteristic authority and presence.

Part of Oxford University, where Raleigh studied but did not gain his degree.

London

By 1575, Raleigh was enrolled in the Inns of Court in London, a training college for the law. It was known as the third university of England (after Oxford and Cambridge) as, apart from law, students also learned history and foreign languages. Raleigh was not a good student: he was too interested in advancing his career to study. (At his trial for **treason** in 1603 he claimed never to have read a word of law!) However, he did have his first poem published in 1576.

Call of the sea

Raleigh started to move in important circles. In Elizabethan England, the arts and sciences were not divided subjects as they are now: an accomplished explorer might also be a poet; a gifted scientist might also be a soldier. Raleigh was much impressed by the **magus** John Dee, an expert on navigation and the greatest mathematician of the age.

Doctor John Dee was a scientist, geographer and mathematician. He gave frequent sailing and navigation advice to Raleigh.

In 1578, Raleigh's half-brother Humphrey Gilbert launched an expedition to establish an English colony in North America. Raleigh was appointed captain of a ship, the *Falcon*. A small vessel (for crossing the Atlantic), she was only 100 tonnes and lightly armed.

The expedition was a disaster. Bad planning, bad weather and bad luck (which was to haunt Gilbert all his life) meant that the *Falcon* only made it as far as the Cape Verde islands. Then she was forced back to Plymouth by aggressive Spanish ships, and by dwindling stores.

YOU CAN FOLLOW RALEIGH'S JOURNEY ON THE FALCON ON THE MAP ON PAGES 42–3.

Slaughter and court manners

Raleigh was beginning to move at the edges of the great, glittering **court** of Elizabeth I. Court life was full of disputes between proud, easily offended **courtiers**. Petty squabbles could easily end in exile, duels or death. Raleigh found himself accidentally caught up in a dangerous dispute between the Earl of Oxford and other powerful courtiers. Raleigh had been trying to work his way into the earl's social and political circle, as **patronage** and the friendship of men in power were the ways to get on at court. Raleigh realized he was out of his depth and needed to find a way out. He accepted a **commission** in the army and was sent to Ireland to put down a rebellion.

Ireland

The English had attempted to subdue and colonize Ireland for centuries, but most of the country was still ruled by tribal chiefs. The English despised the Irish, and considered their manners, language and way of dress to be barbaric. The Irish preferred **Catholicism** to the **Protestant** faith, and Catholic powers such as Spain and France saw Ireland as a backdoor to invading England.

Humphrey Gilbert and Raleigh's cousins Peter and George Carew were already in Ireland. Peter was murdered in an ambush and George only just escaped. Gilbert was conducting a campaign of terror to destroy the Irish rebels, who were being supported by Catholic troops from Spain.

A contemporary engraving of English soldiers going to fight the Irish rebels. Notice the woman at the end of the column: an 'army wife' with children, accompanying her husband to war. She could help by carrying his weapons when he was tired!

When Irish and Spanish troops defending Smerwick Castle surrendered to the English, they were killed. Civilians and women were not spared. Raleigh played a leading part in the slaughter. The Smerwick massacre shocked Europe, but Raleigh claimed he was proud of what he had done.

Return to court

Raleigh was 28 years old, tall, handsome and with a reputation for daring. He returned to court in London, writing letters suggesting ways of governing Ireland that made him sound like an experienced politician and soldier. Raleigh's plan was to become the Queen's favourite, and to make himself into the perfect, well-mannered Protestant gentleman at court.

Queen Elizabeth I, in Raleigh's lifetime one of the most powerful women in the world.

GLORIANA

Queen Elizabeth I never married, but had a string of favourites at court – young men who praised her beauty and intelligence in songs, and complimented her by giving her names such as the 'Faerie Queene' and 'Gloriana'. These men offered undying **courtly love** to the Queen, but this took an artistic form and was a sort of game of flattery and praise. They were rewarded with enormous 'favours': riches and titles. However, being a favourite of the Queen was very dangerous because you made many enemies among the other, envious courtiers.

The Queen's new favourite

In 1580, Raleigh's attempts to become a great and sophisticated **courtier** began to be noticed by the Queen. Her previous favourite, Robert Dudley, Earl of Leicester, found himself replaced by the dashing young Devon sea captain and soldier. Around this time, a story began circulating that Raleigh had spread his expensive cloak over a puddle where the Queen had to walk. Whether or not this actually happened, it shows how Raleigh was seen as gallant and paying attention to the Queen. She wrote to his commanding officers in Ireland, saying that she wished him to remain at **court**.

A FUTURE RIVAL?

In 1584, the Queen's old favourite, Leicester, brought his stepson, Robert Devereux, Earl of Essex, to court. Just seventeen, he was too young to be a rival to Raleigh for the Queen's affection. But Raleigh quite rightly sensed a future rival. Devereux was tall, handsome, intelligent and eager for success, just like Raleigh when he first came to court.

Before Raleigh, Robert Dudley, Earl of Leicester, was the Queen's favourite. He seemed to have such influence over her that he was known as 'the king that is to be'.

Elizabeth I being carried through the streets of London by her finely dressed courtiers. The extravagance and splendour of her court contrasted with the terrible poverty in which many of her subjects lived.

The Queen's favour

Through the early 1580s Raleigh was at the Queen's side as much as it was proper for a courtier to be. He wrote her poems of **courtly love**. These were elegant, intellectual poems praising her beauty, character, power, and so on. In return, the Queen lavished favours such as **monopolies** on Raleigh.

Counting the cost

Being a successful courtier was not all profit. As the Queen's favourite, it cost a fantastic amount for Raleigh to dress in every latest style and to attend and host the lavish balls and banquets that the court indulged in. Many courtiers had very little to do: they might wait years to be given a post as **ambassador** or the command of a fleet. All the time they were at court they had to display wealth and taste.

Hatred of Raleigh

Elizabeth granted Raleigh a hugely profitable monopoly, the 'farm of wines'. This was the right to charge innkeepers for selling wines that Raleigh's agents supposedly checked for quality. Raleigh had also been given a great house, almost a palace, beside the Thames in London 'for the term of the royal pleasure' (as long as the Queen wished). Durham House was Raleigh's home for many years. Ordinary people saw a man dressed lavishly, living in a palace, charging them taxes. They hated him but he chose to ignore them. Instead, he gathered round him at Durham House some of the greatest minds of the age, including the **magus** John Dee, the mathematician Thomas Harriot and the political thinker Richard Hakluyt.

Raleigh had been planning an expedition to colonize the east coast of North America with English settlers since 1583. The Spanish were already in Florida, so he aimed at finding a spot further north. He would call this colony Virginia, in honour of the 'virgin Queen' (as the unmarried Elizabeth was known). Elizabeth approved the plan, but ordered her favourite to stay in England with her! Perhaps as compensation for missing the adventure, he was granted a 17,000-hectare estate in Ireland (of land seized from the Irish). As a further honour, in 1585, the Queen granted him a knighthood and he became Sir Walter Raleigh.

Planning

Raleigh was not planning a simple voyage of exploration but the start of a new English empire in North America, one in which he would have a prominent role. He also knew a colony would make a good base for his **privateers** to attack Spanish treasure galleons! He assembled experts and thinkers at Durham House to plan the expedition.
Thomas Harriot, a brilliant mathematician, had already been to America and set about learning the native American **Algonquian** language. John White would be the expedition's artist.

John White, the expedition's artist, painted very skilful and sympathetic pictures of the Algonquians. He did not try to make them out to be savages, but people from another culture worthy of study and respect.

Setting sail

Raleigh sent out a small reconnaissance expedition to North America in 1584. They returned to England with two Algonquians. Everything that had happened and been learned on the expedition was studied by Raleigh and the men gathered at Durham House.

On 9 April 1585, five ships with 600 men aboard – sailors, soldiers and colonists – sailed from Plymouth, led by Richard Grenville. Raleigh obeyed the Queen and remained at her **court** in London. The ships separated before they even arrived in America, partly because several captains went looking for Spanish ships to plunder.

On 11 July, Grenville landed the colonists. Their meetings with the Indians were friendly, in accord with the ideas of the English lawyer Richard Hakluyt. They discovered the Algonquian practice of smoking tobacco and some of the expedition took this habit up with enthusiasm.

A portrait of Sir Richard Grenville. He was a cousin of Raleigh's, and when Queen Elizabeth would not allow Raleigh to sail on the expedition to North America, Grenville went instead.

HAKLUYT THE HUMANITARIAN

The writings of Richard Hakluyt were studied carefully at Durham House. Hakluyt thought that the problems the Spanish had in their colonies were a direct result of the violence with which they pursued gold and other treasure. The English expedition therefore did not set out to grab wealth, but instead to settle a colony that would live beside the **indigenous** Algonquian Indians. However, Hakluyt did think the Algonquians should convert to the **Protestant** faith.

YOU CAN FOLLOW GRENVILLE'S EXPEDITION ON THE MAP ON PAGES 42–3.

In August 1585, Richard Grenville returned to England, leaving just over 100 men on Roanoke Island, off the coast of Virginia. Ralph Lane, one of Raleigh's trusted officers, was in charge.

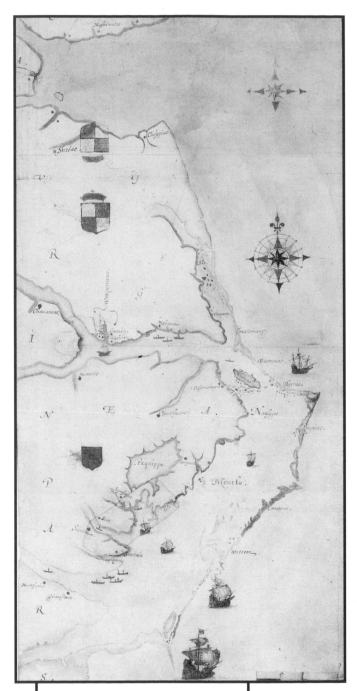

Map of the coast of America where Raleigh settled his colony. This map was drawn by John White, the artist on Raleigh's expedition.

Living off the Indians

The colonists lacked the skills to grow or catch enough food to feed themselves. The local **Algonquian** chief, Wingina, was constantly asked to provide food. Relations between his people and the English seemed good, but there may have been another explanation for why Wingina may have been prepared to share his food. Before the main fleet left for England, a captain had his silver cup stolen by some Algonquians. When they did not return it, he burnt their village and crops. The English may have been more humanitarian than the Spanish, but they never let anyone forget how ruthless they could be.

Harriot's report

Thomas Harriot was interested in learning Algonquian beliefs. The Algonquians told him they had many small gods, but one great god, and that they believed in an afterlife with a heaven and a hell. Harriot described them in his report for Raleigh as a cultured people whose beliefs were close to those of the **Protestant** English.

In this portrait, Raleigh stands with his hand grasping a globe, as though he could hold the whole world in his hand.

The end of the colony

The colony was failing. Wingina, tired of supplying the colonists, planned to attack them, but the English attacked first and Wingina was killed. Tensions between the colonists and **indigenous** people rose dramatically.

On the high seas, there was now an undeclared war between England and Spain. This prevented supply ships from reaching Roanoke until 8 June 1586. They were commanded by another famous Devon sailor, Francis Drake, who was in the area to attack the Spanish in the West Indies.

Drake found the colonists desperate to return home. They had been promised the chance of riches, but instead were living miserably. Lane, scared of failing, reluctantly agreed to send home the weak and sick. But soon he, too, abandoned Roanoke Island. The careful records that Harriot and White had made for Raleigh were tossed overboard by sailors who said the ship was weighed down by them. It was a bitter end to Raleigh's dream of Virginia.

THE IMPORTANCE OF THE COLONY

Although the colony failed, it did achieve some aims. The maps that Harriot and White made on journeys towards the Chesapeake Bay were the first ever maps of this part of North America. Back in England, Raleigh persuaded the Queen to recognize the value of properly supported 'official' colonization, rather than quick dashes for treasure to the New World. Raleigh thus established a pattern for Britain's successful colonies all over North America.

Raleigh had put a lot of money into the expedition to establish a colony. He had paid for ships, supplies and equipment. To make more money, his **monopolies** took vast sums out of the pockets of ordinary people. One observer called him 'the best hated man in the world'.

Robert Devereux, Earl of Essex, Raleigh's rival for the Queen's affections.

Essex's outburst

The Queen made Raleigh Captain of the Guard, a well-paid and important post. He commanded the Queen's personal bodyguards. Robert Devereux, Earl of Essex, was eager to replace Raleigh as the Queen's favourite. He quarrelled with Raleigh, but in the process he also started a quarrel with Elizabeth. At first she was amused; then she became furious and Essex fled. He dashed to the coast to escape the Queen's anger, but then she sent a message saying she had forgiven him. Raleigh now had a serious rival for Elizabeth's attention.

Virginia again

Raleigh planned and paid for another voyage to establish a colony in Virginia. The Queen again refused to let him go on the dangerous voyage to North America. John White was grandly appointed Governor of the Virginian colony, which Raleigh publicly announced would be 'the city of Raleigh'.

In May 1587, three small ships set out. White had no control at sea over the captains: they diverted on **privateering** excursions, ignoring Raleigh's orders to stay together. When they finally arrived at Roanoke Island, the colonists were virtually tricked into leaving the ships, which then quickly sailed away, leaving just one small vessel. The colonists were stranded with few supplies.

The lost colony

After a few months, White made a perilous voyage back to England to plead for help. But the Spanish **Armada** threatened, and no one wanted to spare ships to rescue a few colonists. In April 1588, Raleigh sent two further ships to re-supply the colonists, but again the captains took to privateering, were attacked and forced to return to England. It was not until 1590 that two ships finally did what they were ordered and returned to Roanoke. The colony was deserted. Rumours later came of English people inter-marrying with Indians and living happily further up the coast, but they were never actually seen again.

PRIVATEERING

Privateers were ships that attacked merchant vessels and stole their cargoes. They were like official **pirates**: they had licences from the Queen giving them permission to plunder, so long as the ships attacked were from countries considered enemies.

Privateering made huge profits for English ship owners and crews. In Elizabeth's time there was only a small Royal Navy. In times of war, private captains supplied their own ships to fight alongside the Navy vessels. In return they expected to be licensed to go off privateering. Pirates were outlaws, but privateers were considered loyal citizens.

This engraving is a 19th century depiction of a 16th century 'Brother of the Coast' – one of thousands of European pirates who set up business in the Americas.

The Spanish Armada

The defeat of the **Armada**, the biggest naval fleet Europe had ever seen, is one of the great stories in British seafaring. Raleigh played a key part as one of the commanders of the British forces.

Spain had been fighting an undeclared war with England since 1585. In May 1588, 20,000 Spanish soldiers and over 10,000 sailors put to sea in 130 ships.

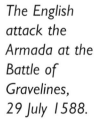

YOU CAN LOCATE THE PLACES MENTIONED ON THE MAP ON PAGES 42–3.

Preparations for invasion

Fleets sailed slowly, so English spies had brought news of the Armada's approach back to London long before it was seen in the English Channel. The Spanish would sail past the **West Country** coast. Lord Howard was 'Lord High Admiral' in command of the English Navy. Raleigh was appointed a Vice-Admiral based in Plymouth, Devon. He told a council of war that although Spanish ships were huge and powerfully armed, English ships were faster. Their tactics should be to fight and flee rapidly, and not engage in lengthy battles. In this way, they damaged several Spanish warships which passed the West Country coast.

The English attack the Armada at the Battle of Gravelines, 29 July 1588.

Fire ships

Sea battles were as much about using the wind to gain advantage as fighting. Raleigh boarded his flagship, the *Ark Royal*, and joined approximately 30 other English ships in the Channel. The English were heavily outnumbered.

The Armada was anchored off the French port of Calais, awaiting reinforcements. On Sunday night, 28 July 1588, the English set fire to some of their ships and set them drifting into the enemy. The Spanish were thrown into confusion. Burning galleons crashed into one another, while the English watched. The next day English ships attacked the surviving Spanish vessels. Many were sunk. Others fled, trying to sail right round Britain, in stormy conditions, to land and seek help from **Catholics** in Scotland or Ireland. Thousands of men were shipwrecked and drowned on the Irish coast. Raleigh became a national hero.

In Raleigh's own words: the defeat of the Armada

'[the Spanish] navy which they termed invincible, consisting of two hundred forty sail of ships … strengthened with Portugal carracks, Florentines, and huge hulks [various types of fighting ships] of other countries: were by thirty of her Majesty's own ships of war, and a few of our own merchant … beaten and shuffled together … and from Calais driven with squibs [fire ships] from their anchors: were chased out of sight of England, round about Scotland and Ireland: a great part of them were crushed against the rocks, and those other that landed, being very many in number, were not withstanding broken, slain, and taken, and so sent from village to village coupled in halters [chains] to be shipped into England.'

(From Raleigh's journal)

Many fleeing Armada ships were wrecked on the rocky coast of Ireland. Hundreds of Spanish sailors drowned in sight of land.

Secret love

Elizabeth ('Bess') Throckmorton, who became Lady Raleigh when her husband was knighted.

In 1584, a young woman called Elizabeth Throckmorton became one of the Queen's 'Maids of the Privy Chamber'. The Queen demanded that her servants should be as remote from men as herself. When she discovered that another maid had secretly married, she attacked her and broke her finger. If male **courtiers** married without permission, they could well end up in the dreaded **Tower of London**.

Like Raleigh, 'Bess' Throckmorton was from a 'gentleman's family' rather than the wealthy **aristocracy**. Some time after her arrival at **court** she and Raleigh became secret lovers. In 1591 she discovered she was pregnant with his child. They married without the Queen's permission.

Enemies

Raleigh was still the Queen's favourite, but this was gaining him more enemies at court. They wanted to blacken his name, and the best way to do this was to suggest that he was not a God-fearing **Protestant** – that in fact he did not believe in God at all. In an age when you could be burned alive for the wrong sort of religious belief, this charge threatened terrible consequences for Raleigh.

In fact, the accusation had followed reports about the conversations that took place at Durham House. Raleigh had gathered about him men who wanted to ask questions about science and ways of thinking. When spies heard about the discussions, they brought all the guests in for questioning before churchmen. Even Harriot's study of the stars from a tower in Durham House was suspicious to Raleigh's enemies.

Dangerous friends

Many of the Durham House group were hated by **traditionalists**. One of the group, an aristocrat named Henry Percy, Earl of Northumberland, was known by his enemies as the 'wizard earl' just because he was interested in manuscripts about unusual spiritual beliefs. Most dangerous of all to the traditionalists was Raleigh's friendship with one of the most brilliant and outspoken **dramatists** of the Elizabethan age, Christopher Marlowe.

Pamphlets were published by Raleigh's enemies claiming that the Durham House group did not believe in God and were 'conjurors'. But Raleigh was still the Queen's favourite. Instead of casting him out of court, she agreed to a request he made for the right to claim a Dorset estate, Sherborne Castle, from the church.

Raleigh chose this castle at Sherborne to be his country home. It was conveniently located between London and Devon.

The Tower

This portrait of Elizabeth I was painted to celebrate the defeat of the Armada. It shows the Queen as an older woman, proud and invincible.

Attacking the Spanish

Spain could build huge navies because she controlled gold and silver mines in Central America that could pay for the ships. Treasure **convoys** sailed back to Spain twice a year, guarded by enormous fighting galleons. In 1591, Raleigh and the Queen put up money to assemble a fleet to attack the autumn convoy. Raleigh hoped to sail, but as usual the Queen wanted him to stay at **court**. His place was taken by his cousin, Richard Grenville.

The fight at the Azores

The expedition failed and Grenville's small ship, the *Revenge*, was attacked and finally sunk by a fleet of powerful Spanish ships. Raleigh gathered reports from survivors and wrote a poetic description of the defeat.

He turned it into a triumph of English bravery:

'All the powder of the *Revenge* to the last barrel was now spent, all her **pikes** broken, forty of her best men slain, and the most part of the rest hurt ... the Revenge not able to move one way or another ... Sir Richard commanded the master gunner to split and sink the ship, that thereby nothing might remain of glory or victory to the Spaniards.'

Another English fleet was sent to **privateer** and capture Spanish treasure ships. Raleigh again put in money, and this time was allowed to sail, but he had only been at sea a short time when a fateful message came recalling him to the Queen. In March 1592 Bess had given birth to a son named Damerei. The Queen was furious and in August had them imprisoned in the **Tower of London**. Nothing more is known of Damerei. It is thought he died as a baby. Raleigh and Bess were kept (separately) in the Tower until December 1592. Raleigh had fallen from grace with the Queen. He felt humbled, and bitter because he had been busy working for his country in the years since the defeat of the **Armada**.

RALEIGH, THE SAILOR'S HERO

While Raleigh was in the Tower, a Spanish treasure ship with a hugely valuable cargo was captured and brought into Dartmouth, Devon. The cargo was being stolen, the Queen herself being cheated. The only man thought able to stop this was Raleigh. So, he was taken under escort to Devon, where his guards were shocked to see him receive, especially from the **West Country** sailors, a hero's welcome.

The harbour at Dartmouth, now full of yachts, where the Spanish treasure ship was taken and stripped of its hugely valuable cargo by local people.

Raleigh and Bess left London and the **court** after their release from the **Tower** to lead a quiet life in the country at Sherborne Castle. Their second son, Wat, was born there in November 1593. In the meantime, Raleigh had been becoming interested in the 'myth of El Dorado', the legend of a golden city hidden in the jungles of South America.

Conquistadors

Spanish conquistadors (soldier-explorers) had conquered parts of north-east South America. They had 'discovered' **indigenous** peoples, such as the Incas of the Andes mountains, who were rich in gold and silver. These treasures were seized and sent back to Spain in **convoys**. These were the ships English **privateers** often attacked. The treasure they captured led to the myth of El Dorado taking hold in English imaginations. By Raleigh's time, gold and silver from the Americas were creating huge wealth for Spain.

The origins of the myth

The Spanish explorer Gonzalo Quesada (c.1497–1579) had claimed what is now Colombia for Spain. He named the territory New Grenada. It was from here that a myth developed that there was, somewhere deep in the jungle, up the great Orinoco River, a city 'made of gold'.

Expeditions would have had to search through dense, unexplored Orinoco rainforest like this to find the mythical city of El Dorado.

El Dorado, the golden king, being 'dusted with gold'.

Like many myths, the details were vague and varied depending on the storyteller. 'El Dorado' is Spanish for 'the one covered in gold'. It was claimed that the ruler of this city, also called El Dorado, had his body dusted with powdered gold every day. At night he just washed it off! Expeditions were sent out to find this mythical city. None of course did. It was believed to lie somewhere near Lake Guatavita.

Raleigh and the myth

It is unlikely that the man who had gathered the Durham House group of thinkers around him believed literally in this myth. However, Raleigh was an adventurer. He was very interested in the idea of gold coming out of the South American jungles. He began to plan an expedition, but it was a mine, not a city, that he was aiming for. He had seen with his own eyes the treasure on captured Spanish ships, and knew that they must be mining huge quantities of gold somewhere in South America.

YOU CAN FOLLOW RALEIGH'S ROUTE ON THE MAP ON PAGES 42–3.

Raleigh also knew the idea of a hidden golden city would appeal to common (and greedy!) people. He was therefore happy to associate the myth of El Dorado with his practical plans to sail down to the coast of Guiana (modern-day Venezuela – not Guyana, which lies further south below the Orinoco delta) and then up the Orinoco River in search of a gold mine. Raleigh was out of favour at court and desperately needed a great success.

... And the reality

You can follow Raleigh's route on the map on pages 42–3.

In February 1595, Raleigh set sail on his long-planned voyage, attracting much attention at **court**. The romance of searching for a source of hidden treasure appealed to Raleigh much more than **privateering**. He was in command of five ships. It was the first time he had personally led an expedition in fifteen years.

In April, the ships arrived at the Caribbean island of Trinidad, less than 32 kilometres (20 miles) off the coast of South America, near the mouth of the great, uncharted Orinoco River. After mapping some of Trinidad's coastline, the ships began their slow journey upstream.

While members of his crew mapped the river and made records of the animals and plants they found, Raleigh wrote a much more poetic account of Guiana. He was captivated by the beauty of what he saw, and became more convinced that gold must lie somewhere upstream.

Two things encouraged his belief in fabulous wealth hidden in the jungle. The river had stones in it that shone and gleamed like gold, although they actually contained only **quartz** and **marcasite**. And **indigenous** people he met on the river told him that there were cities of gold further upstream in the jungle (perhaps to hurry him away from the part where they lived!).

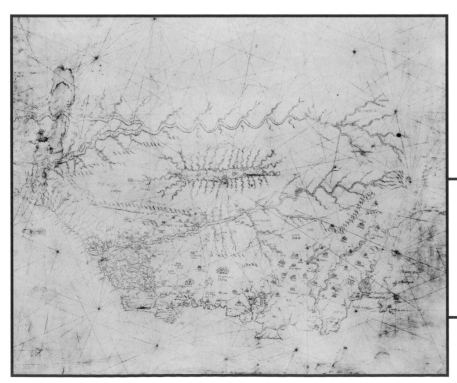

Part of the map made by Raleigh's expedition. The lake with all the tributaries does not in fact exist.

Paradise or publicity?

Raleigh made the land they sailed through sound much more of a paradise than it really was, in the hope of raising support back in England for further expeditions. In fact, the ship's crews were suffering and dying from tropical diseases and the usual illnesses of long sea voyages, such as scurvy, which was caused by a lack of fresh food, expecially fruit and vegetables. There was no city of gold, not even a gold mine, hidden in the jungle. On 14 June 1595 they turned for home, empty-handed.

In Raleigh's words: the Orinoco

'I never saw a more beautiful country, nor more lively prospects: hills so raised here and there over the valleys, the river winding into divers branches; the plains adjoining without bush or stubble, all fair green grass; the ground of hard sand, easy to march on either for horse or foot; the deer crossing every path; the birds, towards the evening, singing on every tree with a thousand several tunes; cranes and herons of white, crimson and carnation perching on the river's side; the air fresh with a gentle easterly wind; and every stone that we stooped to take up promised either gold or silver by his complexion.'

(From Raleigh's journal of the voyage)

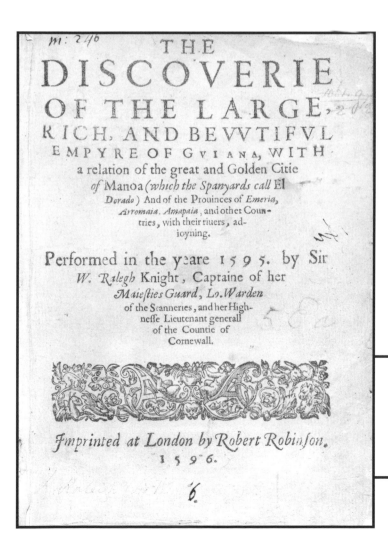

The title page of Raleigh's book on Guiana. It mentions 'El Dorado', although the expedition found no trace of this mythical city.

Despite publication of Raleigh's glowing account of Guiana in 1596 on his return to England, there was little support for further expeditions to search for 'El Dorado'. Raleigh's expedition had not actually brought back anything of worth; it was said he had given away more gold, in the form of gold coins with the Queen's head on them, than he had found!

Disbelieved

Raleigh foolishly made public tales he claimed to have been told about strange, headless warriors, the 'Ewaipanoma', 'with eyes in their shoulders and their mouths in the middle of their breasts', and of tribes who lived in nests in the trees. (This is partly true: some tribes did move their dwellings into trees when the Orinoco River flooded.) Enemies claimed Raleigh had not been to Guiana at all, but had hidden his ships in a remote Cornish cove. They ignored his enlightened ideas for a colony that would work in harmony with the native population, rather than subduing it.

Raleigh foolishly re-told tales he had heard of the 'Ewaipanoma', the people with no heads.

People were beginning to consider the El Dorado myth more rationally. Tales such as this, shared by sailors as they sailed along the unexplored coasts of South America, began to sound ridiculous back in 'sophisticated' London.

An 18th century painting depicting a battle between the English and Spanish navies in the 16th century.

Cadiz

Raleigh's dreams of further exploration were pushed aside by continuing threats of a Spanish invasion. In 1596, Spain was preparing another great **Armada**. English military leaders planned to attack them first, at the Spanish port of Cadiz. Raleigh was to be one of the commanders, his old rival Essex another.

Although the Cadiz attack was a success, endless squabbling between the commanders meant that many things went wrong. Dozens of soldiers wearing heavy metal armour drowned when they were forced to attempt a landing in rough seas. British ships literally barged about, competing for positions to attack. The Spanish had time to sink a **convoy** of their own treasure ships to stop the English getting the cargoes. Cadiz was burned and the British thought they had taught the Spanish a lesson, but the hoped-for profit from captured treasure was lost.

Wounds

Raleigh was wounded in the leg during the raid. In 1597, with Spain again threatening England, another fleet under the same bickering commanders went to attack Spanish ships in the Azores. Raleigh was under the command of Essex, and when Raleigh acted without orders (he used sailors rather than Essex's soldiers to mount a land attack) he was heavily criticized, even though his attack on the town of Fayal was successful and he was wounded several times.

YOU CAN LOCATE CADIZ AND THE AZORE ISLANDS ON THE MAP ON PAGES 42–3.

Raleigh was in his late forties. He walked with a stick because of leg wounds suffered at Cadiz and the Azores. A man with less pride might have seen that the world around him was changing. The Queen just about tolerated him at **court**, but she was close to death.

King James 1, a very different monarch from Elizabeth.

James I

Queen Elizabeth died on 24 March 1603. She had no direct heir, but within a few hours the **Privy Council** had declared James VI of Scotland to be James I of England.

As James made his way south from Scotland he stopped off at the city of Durham and was a guest of the Bishop there. James promised to return Durham House in London, originally the Bishop's property, to him. After 20 years there, Raleigh was given 3 weeks to get out.

This was just the beginning of Raleigh's troubles. Within days he was replaced as Captain of the Guard. Then James revoked all Raleigh's profitable **monopolies**.

A plot against James

As part of his new regime, James wanted peace with the Spanish, but Raleigh, sticking to his long-held views, offered to raise an army to fight them.

The **Protestant** James had been King of England for three months when a **Catholic** plot against him was discovered. One of the conspirators was Raleigh's close friend, Lord Cobham. Raleigh was arrested and accused of involvement in the plot. He denied the charge, and probably knew nothing about it. Nevertheless, he was found guilty of 'horrible **treasons**' by the **Attorney General** and was sentenced to death.

Raleigh watched from his prison window while a conspirator was beheaded. But James suddenly decided to spare Raleigh. He was to be imprisoned indefinitely in the **Tower of London**. In law, he was a 'dead man', with no rights and a suspended (not cancelled) death sentence hanging over his head.

The Tower of London, where noble prisoners condemned to death were beheaded, but common prisoners, like Raleigh, were hanged.

In their own words: Raleigh's trial

Raleigh: *'Here is no treason of mine done. If my Lord Cobham be a traitor, what is that to me?'*

Attorney General: *'All that he did was at thy instigation, thou viper, ... thou traitor! I will prove thee the rankest traitor in all England.'*

Raleigh: *'Master Attorney, I am no traitor. Whether I live or die, I shall stand as true a subject as ever the King hath. You may call me a traitor at your pleasure; yet it becomes not a man of quality or virtue to do so.'*

(From the transcript of the trial made by the court officials)

Return to the Orinoco

The rooms where Raleigh was imprisoned. He also had a garden with a shed where he conducted various experiments and created medicines. His meals were brought in from inns nearby, together with ale and wine.

Raleigh spent thirteen years in the **Tower**. The conditions were not bad: he had two servants and his wife Bess often stayed. The door to his rooms was often unlocked during the day. Bess rented a house nearby, where their third son, Carew, was born in 1605.

Raleigh wrote his *Historie of the World*, which tried to link Bible stories into recorded history. It is a huge book, full of unusual opinions. It was published in 1614.

A popular prisoner

Now he no longer imposed hated **monopolies**, Raleigh was something of a popular figure, if not a hero. (A crowd would gather most days just to watch him take his exercise on the wall of the fortress.) He reminded ordinary people of the glory of Elizabeth's reign. James's queen became a close friend. James's son, the Prince of Wales, adored Raleigh and visited him in the Tower. He once said angrily, 'No one but my father would keep such a bird in a cage'.

Release

Raleigh kept alive the idea of starting English colonies in Virginia and of finding a gold mine on the Orinoco River. After all, the Spanish were still mining masses of gold. Eventually, Raleigh persuaded Parliament and James to let him mount another expedition to explore Guiana for gold.

At sea again

Raleigh was released, but not pardoned, in March 1616. Within days he ordered a ship, the *Destiny*, to be built for the voyage. After careful planning, the expedition left Plymouth in June 1617.

Raleigh had strict orders from James not to attack the Spanish, but clearly had his own ideas. He landed in Ireland, stayed two months, then set sail again with thirteen ships and a thousand men. Raleigh's ships had only sailed as far as the Canaries when they were involved in a skirmish with the Spanish.

Reports

By November they were off the coast of South America. Raleigh was now in his sixties, and suffering from various illnesses. Younger men were more suited to such dangerous voyages as this.

James received conflicting expedition reports: some said that Raleigh had turned **pirate**, others that 'he was already within the bowels of the golden mines ...'.

Given that the Spanish were so established in Guiana, it is hard to see how James expected Raleigh to achieve success without causing trouble. Perhaps he had been allowed to sail just so that he would fail.

YOU CAN FOLLOW RALEIGH'S ROUTE ON THE MAP ON PAGES 42–3.

Raleigh's ships sailed in vain up this river, the Orinoco, in search of Spanish gold mines.

The Spanish complained bitterly to James about Raleigh's voyage, saying the mine he sought lay in territory claimed by Spain. James, keen to keep friendly links with Spain, said that if Raleigh attacked Spanish interests he would send him to Madrid for execution.

Raleigh's eldest son Wat was on the expedition. He and a captain, Laurence Keymis, led an exploring party up the Orinoco while the rest of the expedition, badly weakened by disease, anchored off the coast. Raleigh had said his crews were the 'scum of the earth', and he may have wanted them kept well away from the Spanish coastal settlements.

Gold panning in Guiana, drawn in 1599. Europeans were so eager to believe that huge quantities of gold were to be had in South America that they were keen to see pictures like this, even though they might be inaccurate.

The fateful fight

Keymis and Wat stopped outside San Tome, a Spanish village close to where Raleigh claimed the gold mine lay. They did not want to attack the village, but the Spanish sent out a raiding party. In the ensuing fight the Spanish were driven off, but Wat was killed. He was just 24.

Keymis seems to have lost all heart after this. His men made a half-hearted attempt to find the mine, but failed. They burned San Tome, then returned to the main fleet. Raleigh was horrified by what had happened. He told Keymis that he had 'ruined him beyond hope of recovery'. Keymis went to his cabin and shot himself.

YOU CAN FOLLOW THE ROUTE OF RALEIGH'S EXPEDITION ON THE MAP ON PAGES 42–3.

Mutiny

The crews refused to mount a second expedition up the Orinoco. So Raleigh decided to sail up to Virginia hoping to find his lost colony. No other ships would follow him. The once all-powerful Raleigh had lost the power to command. In June 1618, the *Destiny* returned alone to Plymouth.

Raleigh had probably known in his heart that his quest would fail, and before leaving England had secretly set up possible plans for fleeing to a foreign country if things went wrong. He wrote in his journal for March 1618: 'What shall become of me I do not know. I am unpardoned in England, and my poor estate consumed; and whether any other prince or State will give me bread I know not'. In fact, he had already accepted a **commission** in the French navy to use as a means of escape from danger in England.

Raleigh, aged by illness, painted by an unknown artist in 1597.

Raleigh was not arrested immediately when he docked at Plymouth. Popular opinion was against the Spanish, and Raleigh was seen as a fallen hero. James hesitated. Raleigh was at liberty in the **West Country** several weeks before he was arrested by a cousin, Lewis Stuckley. He could easily have escaped abroad with his family, but he seemed to have lost the will to fight. However, on the way to London he faked illness by smearing his skin with an irritant and convincing his guards that he was suffering from a contagious disease. They halted for several weeks at Salisbury. He was buying time to write a full account of what had happened in Guiana.

A portrait of Raleigh and his eldest son, Wat, done when Wat was about eight years old. Raleigh outlived Wat, who was killed in the fight at San Tome, Guiana, in 1618 when he was 24.

A plan too late

Back in London, Raleigh woke up to the danger he faced: his death sentence would surely be carried out. He arranged to flee to France, but a servant betrayed the plan to Stuckley. As Raleigh sailed down the Thames to a waiting French ship, Stuckley intercepted him. (Stuckley was universally loathed and nicknamed '**Judas**' for what he had done to his relation; he died insane.)

The charges

Raleigh's cause was hopeless. He could have been charged with **treason** because he had secretly accepted the French **commission**. He could have been accused of breaking the agreement under which he had been released from the **Tower** because he had attacked the Spanish. James simply revoked the long-standing delay of Raleigh's execution.

A hero to the end

In a private trial, Raleigh was sentenced to death. Many powerful people appealed for mercy, but the King would not listen to them. The only charity Raleigh received was that the sentence should be carried out by beheading, which was quicker than hanging.

On 29 October 1618, Walter Raleigh was executed. When the executioner asked if he wanted a blindfold, Raleigh, ever the hero, replied: 'Think you I fear the shadow of the axe, when I fear not the axe itself?' And when the executioner hesitated, Raleigh uttered his last brave words: 'What does thou fear? Strike, man, strike!'

In Raleigh's own words

On the night before he was executed Raleigh wrote this short poem in his Bible.

'*Even such is time, which takes in trust
Our youth, our joys and all we have,
And pays us but with earth and dust;
Who, in the dark and silent grave,
When we have wandered all our ways
Shuts up the story of our days.
But from this earth, this grave, this dust,
My God shall raise me up, I trust.*'

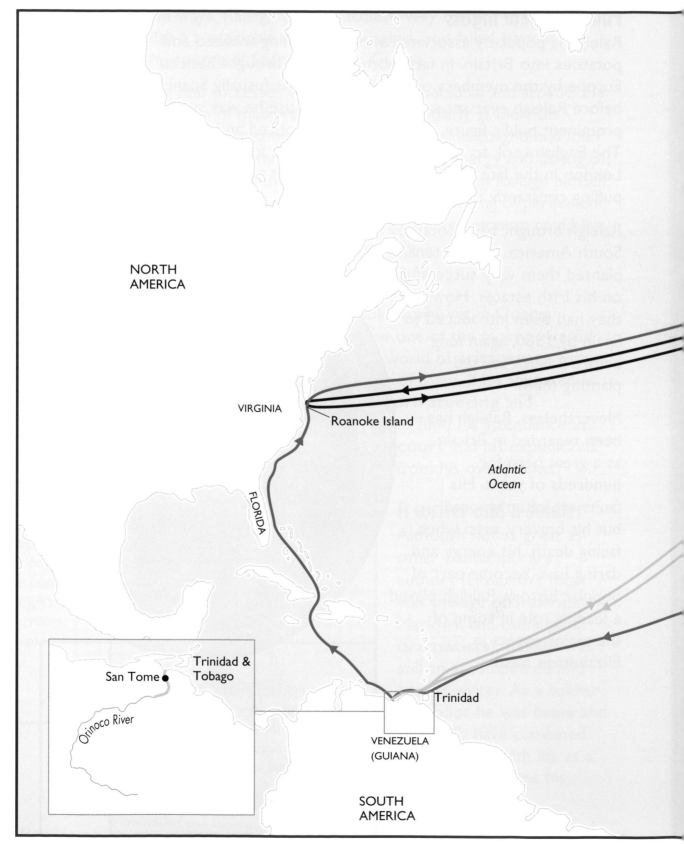

NORTH
AMERICA

VIRGINIA

Roanoke Island

*Atlantic
Ocean*

FLORIDA

Trinidad &
Tobago

San Tome

Orinoco River

Trinidad

VENEZUELA
(GUIANA)

SOUTH
AMERICA

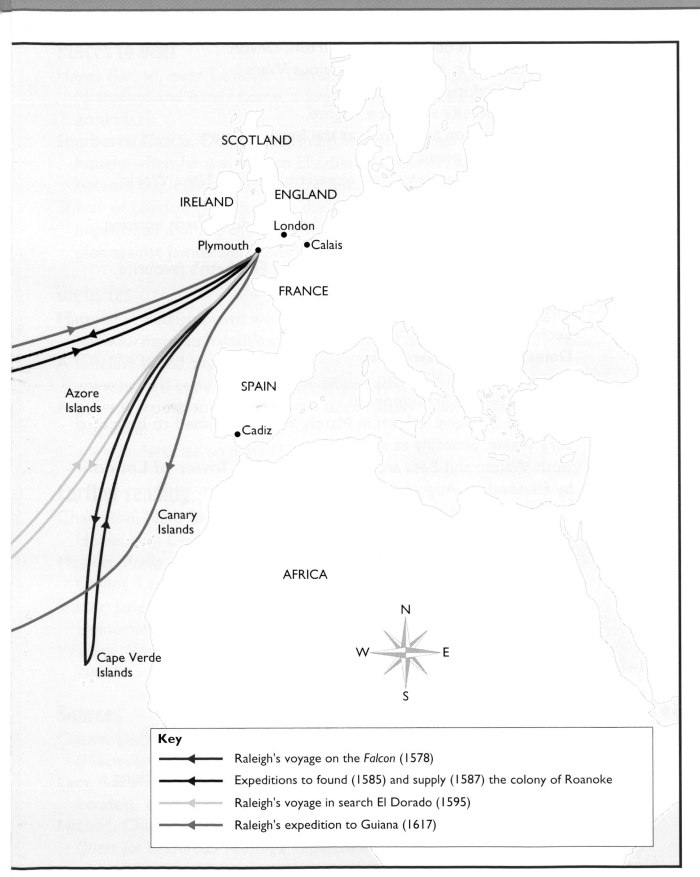

SCOTLAND

IRELAND

ENGLAND

London

●Calais

Plymouth

FRANCE

Azore
Islands

SPAIN

●Cadiz

Canary
Islands

AFRICA

N

W — E

S

Cape Verde
Islands

Key

Raleigh's voyage on the *Falcon* (1578)

Expeditions to found (1585) and supply (1587) the colony of Roanoke

Raleigh's voyage in search El Dorado (1595)

Raleigh's expedition to Guiana (1617)

Glossary

Algonquian Native Americans who live in the area covered by Virginia and Maryland, among other eastern American areas

ambassador representative of one country to another

aristocracy ruling class of England in Raleigh's time, holding family titles granted by previous kings and queens. They were mostly land-owning and immensely wealthy.

Armada Spanish naval invasion fleet

Attorney General the most powerful legal post in Britain, acting for the Crown (the king or queen) in law cases

Catholic member or follower of the Roman Catholic Church, led by the pope in Rome

commission 'naval or military' job appointment as an officer

conquistadors Spanish soldier-explorers who conquered much of South and Central America

convoy group of cargo-carrying vessels sailing together, usually protected by naval ships

court queen or king and her/his circle of attending councillors, advisers, friends and relatives

courtier someone (nearly always male) who attends court, sometimes as an adviser, although often without any real role or purpose there

courtly love a literary style, whereby love poems were written to women of the court (usually the queen) appearing to praise her as a lover. The idea was a refined sort of game (Raleigh was rather good at it): the poet was supposed to show his intelligence, wit and passion, but not actually try to woo the woman.

degree qualification most students gain when they complete their studies at university

dramatist someone who writes plays

indigenous indigenous people are local or 'native' to a particular country or area. They are born in that country usually and have many generations of relatives who were also born there.

Judas the disciple who betrayed Christ to the authorities. His name has become linked (insultingly) to anyone suspected of betrayal.

magus one skilled in astrology and possibly magic

marcasite iron pyrites, a mineral sometimes looking like gold or silver, but which has little value

monopoly form of tax, used by Elizabeth's court to raise money from ordinary people. Monopolies created a duty to be paid for some goods or service.

paragon person or thing of excellence; the best of its type

patronage having the support of someone in a position of authority, who helps you both practically (for example, financially) and by putting you forward to those in power

pike a long, heavy spear, used by marines and soldiers in Raleigh's time

pirates (piracy) ships and crews who illegally attack any other vessels for profit. They were regarded as criminals. A pirate would instantly face death if caught.

privateers (privateering) ships that attack foreign merchant vessels and take their cargo, often paying some of the captured prize to their king or queen. Unlike pirates, privateers claimed only to attack the ships of countries that were 'enemies' of their own nation.

Privy Council most powerful group of advisers in the Royal Court. Raleigh was always annoyed that he was never asked to join Queen Elizabeth's Privy Council, most of whose members were aristocrats.

Protestant member or follower of any western Christian church which supported changes (reformation) in the Roman Catholic Church in the early 16th century

quartz mineral with a shiny appearance

Tower of London fortress in London that was used as a prison for many centuries

traditionalists people who believe in doing things the way they always have been done

treason crime of betraying one's monarch or country, for example by attacking, spying, or plotting against the ruler

West Country all of England roughly south and west of Bristol, that is the counties Somerset, Dorset, Devon and Cornwall